ANNIE OAKLEY

BIOGRAPHY

The Remarkable Life of America's Sharpshooting Star

BRIEF BIO PUBLISHING

Copyright © 2024 BRIEF BIO PUBLISHING

All rights reserved. The stories within these pages are the intellectual property of BRIEF BIO PUBLISHING and are protected by copyright law. No part of this book may be reproduced, shared, or transmitted in any form—digital, mechanical, or otherwise—without the prior written consent of the publisher, except for brief excerpts used for critical reviews or educational purposes.

TABLE OF CONTENT

INTRODUCTION	4
FORMATIVE YEARS	6
PATH TO PROMINENCE	10
LIFE ON THE ROAD	16
MASTERING THE ART OF SHOOTING	25
INTIMATE WORLD	35
ADVOCACY AND IMPACT	45
LATER YEARS AND LEGACY	55
WRAP-UP	64

INTRODUCTION

In the annals of American history, few figures shine as brightly as Annie Oakley—a woman who not only mastered the art of sharpshooting but also shattered the conventions of her time. Born in a humble Ohio cabin in 1860, Annie's journey from poverty to fame is a riveting tale of resilience, talent, and unyielding spirit. With a rifle in hand and a heart full of determination, she captivated audiences across the globe, transforming the perception of women in the late 19th century.

Annie's extraordinary life was more than just a series of breathtaking performances; it was a powerful statement about the strength and capabilities of women. As she took aim at targets, she also aimed to dismantle the stereotypes that confined women to the domestic sphere. With each bullseye, she inspired countless others to break free from societal limitations, proving that skill and ambition know no gender.

This biography explores deep into the life of Annie Oakley, exploring the trials and triumphs that shaped her into the icon she became. From her early struggles in a world that often underestimated her to her dazzling performances alongside the likes of Buffalo Bill, Annie's story is one of grit, grace, and glory.

FORMATIVE YEARS

In the quiet, rolling hills of rural Ohio, a legend was born. Annie Oakley, originally named Phoebe Ann Moses, entered the world on August 13, 1860, into a family of modest means. The daughter of a Quaker farmer, her early life was marked by both hardship and resilience. Born into a turbulent era, Annie's childhood was shaped by the struggles of her family, including the untimely death of her father when she was just six years old. This loss thrust her mother into the role of sole provider, a daunting task that would set the stage for Annie's fierce independence.

From a young age, Annie exhibited a remarkable spirit and an unyielding determination. While other children played with dolls, Annie found solace in the woods, where she learned to hunt and trap small game to help feed her family. Armed with a makeshift rifle, she demonstrated an uncanny ability to hit her targets with precision. It was here, amidst the rustling leaves and the sounds of nature, that the seeds of her extraordinary talent were sown.

Annie's childhood was not without its trials. The family struggled to make ends meet, often relying on the kindness of neighbors and the land for sustenance. Yet, these challenges only fueled her desire to succeed. At the tender age of 15, she took her skills to the next level, entering a shooting contest against a seasoned marksman named Frank Butler. The stakes were high, but Annie's confidence was unwavering. With a steady hand and unwavering focus, she outshot Butler, earning not only a cash prize but also the admiration of the crowd—and the heart of her future husband.

This pivotal moment marked the beginning of a partnership that would propel Annie into the spotlight. Frank recognized her extraordinary talent and became her mentor, guiding her through the intricacies of sharpshooting. Together, they formed an inseparable bond, both personally and professionally. As they traveled the country, performing in various exhibitions, Annie's fame began to grow. Her remarkable ability to hit targets with astonishing accuracy captivated audiences and challenged the norms of a society that often relegated women to the sidelines.

Annie's rise was not merely a personal triumph; it was a revolutionary act. In an age when women were expected to conform to traditional roles, Annie shattered stereotypes with every bullseye she hit. Her performances showcased not only her skill but also her strength and independence. She became a symbol of empowerment for women everywhere, proving that they could excel in fields traditionally dominated by men.

As she honed her craft, Annie also developed a unique style that set her apart from other performers. She wore a tailored outfit that combined practicality with flair, complete with a fringed leather jacket and a wide-brimmed hat. Her stage presence was magnetic, and her infectious smile endeared her to audiences of all ages. With each performance, she drew crowds that marveled at her ability to shoot glass balls mid-air, split playing cards, and even shoot a cigarette from between Frank's lips—an act that would become legendary.

Yet, despite her burgeoning fame, Annie never forgot her roots. She remained grounded, often reflecting on her humble beginnings and the struggles that shaped her. Her early life instilled in her a sense of gratitude and a desire to uplift others. As she gained recognition, she began to advocate for women's rights, using her platform to encourage young girls to pursue their dreams, no matter the obstacles.

PATH TO PROMINENCE

The year was 1885, and the American West was a canvas splashed with adventure, excitement, and the promise of the unknown. It was during this vibrant era that Annie Oakley's life would take a dramatic turn, propelling her from a small-town sharpshooter to a household name. The stage was set for her extraordinary journey, one that would see her defy societal norms and become a symbol of empowerment for women across the nation.

Annie's first taste of fame came when she and her husband, Frank Butler, found themselves performing in a shooting exhibition in Cincinnati. It was here that she caught the eye of none other than William F. "Buffalo Bill" Cody, the legendary showman and founder of the Wild West Show. Impressed by her remarkable talent and stage presence, Cody extended an invitation for Annie to join his traveling spectacle. This was a pivotal moment—one that would change the course of her life forever.

With a mix of excitement and trepidation, Annie stepped into the world of Buffalo Bill's Wild West Show. The show was a dazzling display of cowboy culture, featuring rodeos, reenactments of famous battles, and thrilling acts that showcased the skills of marksmen and women alike. It was a place where legends were born, and Annie was determined to carve her own name into the annals of history.

As she took to the stage, dressed in her iconic fringed attire, Annie quickly became the star of the show. Her performances were nothing short of breathtaking. With every shot fired, she captivated audiences, demonstrating not only her unparalleled accuracy but also her charisma and flair. She could shoot the wings off a fly or hit a dime tossed into the air, and her signature act of shooting glass balls mid-flight left spectators in awe. The audience erupted in applause, and Annie reveled in the energy, her spirit soaring as high as her targets.

But Annie's rise to fame was not merely about her extraordinary talent; it was also about her ability to connect with the audience. She exuded confidence and charm, breaking down barriers that had long confined women to the shadows. In an era when women were often relegated to domestic roles, Annie became a role model, proving that skill and ambition knew no gender. Her performances were not just entertainment; they were a declaration of independence, challenging societal norms and inspiring countless women to pursue their dreams.

As Annie's fame spread, so did her influence. She became a sensation, attracting attention not only for her shooting prowess but also for her captivating personality. Newspapers and magazines clamored to feature her, and she was often hailed as "Little Sure Shot"—a nickname that embodied her extraordinary talent and tenacity. Annie's story resonated with the public; she was not just a performer but a symbol of the American spirit, embodying the ideals of courage, resilience, and the pursuit of excellence.

However, the path to stardom was not without its challenges. As Annie navigated the complexities of fame, she faced the scrutiny of a society that was still grappling with the idea of a woman in the spotlight. Critics questioned her choice to perform, arguing that it was unseemly for a woman to display such prowess in a male-dominated field. Yet, Annie remained undeterred. With the unwavering support of Frank, who stood by her side as both partner and manager, she continued to push boundaries and defy expectations.

Annie's impact extended beyond the stage. She began to use her platform to advocate for women's rights, encouraging young girls to embrace their ambitions and pursue their passions. She famously stated, "I would like to see every girl know how to shoot, and I would like to see every girl have the opportunity to learn." This commitment to empowerment resonated deeply with her audience, further solidifying her status as a trailblazer.

As the Wild West Show traveled across the United States and beyond, Annie Oakley became a household name. From the bustling streets of New York City to the grand theaters of Europe, she dazzled audiences with her skill and charm. Crowds flocked to see the remarkable woman who could shoot with the precision of a master marksman, and her performances became a celebration of both talent and tenacity.

Amidst the whirlwind of fame, Annie remained grounded, never forgetting the struggles of her early life. She often returned to her roots, visiting the small town where she grew up, and she made it a point to give back to the community that had shaped her. Whether it was through charitable donations or mentorship programs, Annie used her success to uplift others, embodying the spirit of generosity that defined her character.

LIFE ON THE ROAD

The roar of the crowd, the scent of gunpowder, and the thrill of adventure became the backdrop of Annie Oakley's life as she embarked on a whirlwind journey across America and beyond. Life on the road with Buffalo Bill's Wild West Show was not just a series of performances; it was a grand odyssey filled with excitement, camaraderie, and the promise of new horizons. For Annie, each destination was a new chapter, and every audience was a fresh canvas upon which she would paint her legacy.

As the Wild West Show traveled from bustling cities to small towns, Annie found herself immersed in the vibrant tapestry of American life. The show was a spectacle unlike any other—a dazzling display of horsemanship, sharpshooting, and reenactments of famous battles that brought the spirit of the frontier to life. With a caravan of colorful wagons, adorned with flags and banners, the troupe made its way across the country, captivating audiences wherever they went.

Annie's days were filled with rehearsals, practice, and preparation for the evening performances. The camaraderie among the performers was palpable, as they shared stories, laughter, and the occasional mischief. They were a family on the road, bound together by their love for the stage and the thrill of adventure. Annie formed deep friendships with her fellow performers, including the legendary sharpshooter and horsewoman Calamity Jane, whose wild spirit matched her own. Together, they forged a bond that transcended the spotlight, supporting one another through the ups and downs of life on the road.

The nights were electric. As the sun dipped below the horizon, the show would come alive with the sounds of cheering crowds and the crack of gunfire. Annie, dressed in her signature outfit, took center stage, her heart racing with anticipation. The thrill of performing never dulled; each show was a new opportunity to dazzle and inspire. The audience, a mix of cowboys, families, and curious onlookers, would hold their breath as she prepared to take aim. With a wink and a smile, she would launch into her act, shooting glass balls, splitting playing cards, and executing her famous trick of shooting a cigarette from Frank's lips—each shot a testament to her extraordinary skill and daring spirit.

But life on the road was not without its challenges. The constant travel took a toll, and the performers faced the rigors of life away from home. Long hours, cramped living quarters, and the ever-present pressure to entertain weighed heavily on them. Annie often missed the comfort of her Ohio roots, the tranquil woods where she first honed her skills. Yet, the thrill of the spotlight and the adoration of her fans fueled her resolve. She embraced the challenges, viewing them as a part of the adventure.

As they traveled, the Wild West Show also encountered a kaleidoscope of cultures and traditions. From the bustling streets of Chicago to the dusty trails of the Southwest, Annie and her fellow performers interacted with diverse communities, learning about their customs and stories. She was particularly fascinated by Native American cultures, and she often sought to understand their perspectives, forging friendships that would last a lifetime. In a time when misconceptions and stereotypes ran rampant, Annie's genuine curiosity and respect for others set her apart as a compassionate figure in a world often divided.

The show's travels also took them overseas, where Annie's fame reached new heights. In 1887, the Wild West Show embarked on a grand tour of Europe, showcasing the spirit of the American frontier to captivated audiences across the Atlantic. From London to Paris, Annie was met with adulation, her performances drawing crowds that marveled at her skill and charisma. The excitement of performing for royalty and dignitaries was exhilarating, but Annie remained humble, always attributing her success to the support of her fellow performers and the love of her fans.

However, the journey was not without its trials. The pressures of fame sometimes led to conflict within the troupe. Jealousy and rivalry bubbled beneath the surface, as some performers struggled to share the spotlight with Annie, whose star continued to rise. Yet, through it all, Annie maintained her grace and composure, refusing to let the negativity dim her spirit. She often reminded her fellow performers that they were all part of something greater—a shared dream of entertaining and inspiring audiences.

One of the most poignant moments during her travels occurred in 1894 when the Wild West Show performed in the heart of Chicago for the World's Fair. The event celebrated innovation and progress, and Annie stood at the forefront, showcasing the skills that had made her a legend. Amidst the grandeur of the fair, she felt a deep sense of pride and gratitude for the journey that had brought her to this moment. The cheers of the crowd echoed in her ears, and she knew that she was not just performing for herself but for every woman who dared to dream beyond societal constraints.

As the years rolled on, life on the road became a tapestry woven with memories of laughter, friendship, and triumph . Each performance was a celebration of resilience, and Annie Oakley became synonymous with the spirit of the Wild West. The stories of her adventures spread like wildfire, inspiring countless individuals to embrace their own passions and pursue their dreams, regardless of the obstacles they faced.

Annie's influence extended beyond the stage; she became a beacon of hope for women everywhere. Her journey was a testament to the power of determination and the belief that one could rise above societal expectations. As she traveled from town to town, she often took time to meet with young girls, sharing her story and encouraging them to take up shooting and other pursuits that were traditionally deemed unsuitable for women. "You can do anything you set your mind to," she would tell them, her eyes sparkling with conviction.

The camaraderie among the performers was a source of strength, and they often celebrated their successes together. After a particularly thrilling show, the troupe would gather around a campfire, sharing stories and laughter under the starlit sky.

These moments of connection were precious, reminding Annie of the importance of friendship and support in the pursuit of their dreams.

Yet, the road was not always smooth. There were moments of doubt and fear, especially when faced with the harsh realities of life on tour. Illness, injuries, and the constant pressure to perform weighed heavily on Annie and her fellow performers. During one grueling tour, Annie fell ill, and the fear of disappointing her fans loomed large. But with the unwavering support of Frank and her fellow performers, she found the strength to push through, proving once again that her spirit was unbreakable.

As the Wild West Show continued to gain popularity, Annie found herself at the center of a cultural phenomenon. She was not just a performer; she was a symbol of the American frontier, embodying the ideals of bravery, independence, and the relentless pursuit of excellence. Her story resonated with audiences far and wide, and she became a household name, celebrated not only for her sharpshooting skills but also for her unwavering spirit.

The thrill of life on the road was matched only by the joy of connecting with her fans. After each performance, Annie would often take the time to meet with audience members, signing autographs and sharing stories. The smiles on their faces fueled her passion, reminding her of the impact she was making. She cherished these interactions, knowing that she was not just entertaining but also inspiring a new generation to break free from the constraints of society.

MASTERING THE ART OF SHOOTING

The sun rose over the horizon, casting a golden hue across the vast expanse of the American West. It was a new day, and for Annie Oakley, it was another opportunity to refine her craft and push the boundaries of what was possible with a rifle. The art of shooting was not merely a skill for Annie; it was a passion, a way of life, and a form of self-expression that would define her legacy. As she prepared for another day of practice, her heart raced with anticipation, ready to embrace the challenges that lay ahead.

Annie's journey to mastery began in her childhood, where she first learned to wield a rifle in the woods of Ohio. But now, as a celebrated sharpshooter, she understood that true mastery required dedication, discipline, and an insatiable thirst for improvement. Every day, she would rise before dawn, the world still cloaked in silence, and make her way to the shooting range. This was her sanctuary, a sacred space where she could connect with her weapon and hone her skills.

With her trusty rifle in hand, Annie would set up an array of targets—glass balls, playing cards, and even tin cans—each representing a new challenge to conquer. She understood that every shot was an opportunity to learn, to adapt, and to grow. As she took her position, she focused her mind, blocking out the distractions of the world around her. The soft rustle of the wind, the distant call of birds, and the rhythmic beat of her own heart became her only companions.

The first shot rang out, echoing across the open expanse. With a crack that split the morning air, the glass ball shattered into a thousand glittering fragments, a testament to her skill and precision. Annie smiled, exhilarated by the thrill of the moment. But she knew that mastery was not just about hitting the target; it was about understanding the nuances of shooting—the balance of her stance, the alignment of her sights, and the gentle squeeze of the trigger. Each shot was a dance, a harmonious interplay between mind and body, and she was determined to perfect every movement.

As the days turned into weeks, Annie pushed herself harder, experimenting with new techniques and challenging herself to take on more difficult shots. She began to incorporate tricks into her routine—shooting while spinning, firing from unusual angles, and even shooting with her left hand. Each new challenge was met with unwavering determination, and she often found herself lost in the thrill of the chase, her heart racing with excitement as she aimed for perfection.

Annie also understood the importance of mental fortitude in her craft. She spent time visualizing her shots, imagining the trajectory of the bullet and the satisfying sound of the target shattering. "Your mind is your greatest weapon," she would often tell herself. "Believe in your ability, and the body will follow." This mental preparation became a vital part of her training, enabling her to remain calm and focused, even in the most high-pressure situations.

As she mastered the technical aspects of shooting, Annie also sought inspiration from the world around her. She would often observe the wildlife in the fields, studying their movements and learning to anticipate their actions. This keen sense of observation translated into her shooting, allowing her to react instinctively and accurately. She became a true student of nature, understanding that every shot was not just a test of skill but a connection to the world around her.

Annie's relentless pursuit of excellence did not go unnoticed. Fellow performers in the

Wild West Show began to admire her dedication and sought her guidance. She welcomed the opportunity to mentor others, sharing her knowledge and passion for shooting with those eager to learn. The camaraderie among the performers grew stronger as they practiced together, pushing each other to new heights. Annie's enthusiasm was infectious, and soon, the shooting range became a hub of excitement and camaraderie, filled with laughter and friendly competition.

One day, during a particularly intense practice session, Frank challenged Annie to a friendly competition. The stakes were high—a dinner of her choice at their favorite restaurant. With a twinkle in her eye, Annie accepted the challenge, knowing that the playful rivalry would only fuel her determination. The two set up a series of targets, each one more difficult than the last. As they took turns shooting, the air was thick with anticipation. The friendly banter and laughter only heightened the stakes, and the tension was palpable.

With each shot fired, Annie felt the thrill of competition coursing through her veins. The sound of bullets striking their targets echoed like music, and the cheers of their fellow performers provided an exhilarating backdrop. As the final round approached, Annie took a deep breath, centering herself. This was not just about winning; it was about the joy of the craft, the thrill of the chase, and the bond she shared with Frank. With a steady hand and unwavering focus, she took her shot, hitting the target with pinpoint accuracy. The crowd erupted in applause, and Frank, ever the good sport, raised his hands in surrender, a wide grin on his face. "You've outdone me again, Annie!" he exclaimed, pulling her into a celebratory embrace. The laughter and cheers of their fellow performers echoed around them, creating a moment of pure joy that solidified their bond even further.

As the days turned into months, Annie's reputation as a sharpshooter continued to grow. She was not just a performer; she was a master of her craft, and her performances became legendary. Audiences flocked to see her, eager to witness the woman who could shoot with such precision and grace. Each show was a spectacle, a blend of skill and showmanship that left spectators breathless. Annie reveled in the energy of the crowd, feeding off their excitement and using it to elevate her performance to new heights.

But with fame came scrutiny. Critics began to take notice, and while many praised her talent, others questioned her methods and the authenticity of her performances. Annie faced these challenges head-on, determined to prove that her skills were the result of hard work and dedication, not mere luck or trickery. She invited skeptics to watch her practice, demonstrating her techniques and sharing her journey. "Shooting is an art," she would say, "and like any art, it requires passion, practice, and perseverance."

In her quest for mastery, Annie also sought to innovate. She began to experiment with different types of firearms, pushing the boundaries of what was possible. She studied the mechanics of each weapon, understanding how to maximize their potential. This exploration led her to develop new tricks and routines that captivated audiences even more. The thrill of the unexpected became a hallmark of her performances, and she delighted in surprising her fans with her ever-evolving skills.

One fateful day, while practicing for an upcoming show, Annie decided to attempt a shot that had never been done before—shooting a target while riding a galloping horse. The idea thrilled her, and she was determined to make it work. With

Frank by her side, she mounted her horse and set up the target a distance away. The adrenaline surged through her as she galloped toward the target, the wind whipping through her hair. With a steady hand and unwavering focus, she took aim and fired. The sound of the shot rang out, and to her amazement, the target shattered into pieces. The exhilaration of the moment was indescribable, and she knew she had just created a new standard for sharpshooting.

As Annie continued to master the art of shooting, she also became an advocate for women in sports. She recognized the barriers that women faced in pursuing their passions and sought to inspire others to break free from societal constraints. She organized shooting clinics for young girls, teaching them the fundamentals of marksmanship and instilling in them the belief that they could achieve anything they set their minds to. "Shooting is for everyone," she would tell them, her eyes shining with conviction. "Don't let anyone tell you otherwise."

Annie's influence extended beyond the shooting range. She became a role model for women everywhere, proving that with determination and hard work, they could excel in any field. Her story resonated with countless individuals, inspiring them to pursue their dreams, regardless of the obstacles they faced. The art of shooting became a symbol of empowerment, and Annie Oakley stood at the forefront, leading the charge.

INTIMATE WORLD

Behind the dazzling performances and the roar of the crowds, Annie Oakley's personal life was a tapestry woven with love, ambition, and the complexities of fame. As she navigated the exhilarating world of sharpshooting and the Wild West Show, she also grappled with the challenges of maintaining a sense of normalcy and intimacy amidst the whirlwind of her public persona. This chapter of her life was as compelling as her performances, filled with moments of joy, heartache, and the unwavering bond she shared with her husband, Frank Butler.

Annie and Frank's love story was one for the ages—a tale of partnership and mutual respect that blossomed against the backdrop of their thrilling lives on the road. They had met in a shooting competition when Annie was just a teenager, and Frank, a seasoned marksman, was immediately taken by her talent and spirit.

Their initial rivalry soon transformed into admiration, and before long, they were inseparable. Frank became not only Annie's husband but also her manager and confidant, supporting her ambitions while navigating the complexities of their shared life.

While the couple reveled in the excitement of their performances, they also cherished their quiet moments together. After long days filled with rehearsals and shows, they would often retreat to the solace of their shared wagon, where they would unwind and reflect on the day's events. These intimate moments were filled with laughter, storytelling, and dreams of the future. Annie would often tease Frank about his own shooting skills, playfully challenging him to improve while he would return the jest, reminding her that even the best sharpshooters had room for improvement. Their playful banter was a testament to their deep bond, a connection that remained strong even amid the chaos of their lives.

Despite their love, the pressures of fame began to take their toll. As Annie's star continued to rise, so did the expectations placed upon her. The public's adoration often felt overwhelming, and the constant travel meant that they were frequently away from home, leaving little time for the couple to nurture their relationship. Annie felt the weight of responsibility on her shoulders; she was not just a performer but a symbol of hope and empowerment for countless women. The desire to inspire others often clashed with her need for personal fulfillment and connection.

One evening, after a particularly grueling week on the road, Annie and Frank found themselves in a quiet town in the Midwest. The show had just concluded, and as the stars twinkled above, they took a stroll through the empty fairgrounds, the echoes of the audience still ringing in their ears.

"Do you ever wish we could just stop for a while?" Annie asked, her voice barely above a whisper. "Just take a break and enjoy life without the spotlight?"

Frank paused, looking at her with a mixture of understanding and concern. "I do, Annie. But we're doing something important. You're changing lives out there. You've inspired so many girls to pick up a rifle and believe in themselves." His words were filled with pride, yet Annie could sense the weight of their shared sacrifices. They had both given so much to their careers, and in that moment, she realized how much she longed for a balance between their public and private lives.

That night, as they settled into their wagon, Annie made a decision. She would take time to nurture her personal life, to embrace the love she shared with Frank amidst the chaos of fame. They began to carve out small moments together—dinners under the stars, quiet evenings spent playing cards, and occasional trips to visit family back in Ohio. These moments became sacred, a reminder of the love that had brought them together in the first place.

However, the road was not without its challenges. The couple faced moments of doubt and insecurity, particularly as they navigated the complexities of fame. Annie often felt the pressure to maintain her image as a flawless sharpshooter, while Frank grappled with his own insecurities as he managed her career. There were nights when the weight of their responsibilities felt too heavy to bear, and the couple would find themselves in heated discussions about their future.

One particularly difficult night, after a show in New York City, Annie confronted Frank about his growing frustration with her rising fame. "You're not just my husband; you're my partner. I need you to be by my side, not just in the spotlight but behind the scenes too," she implored, her voice filled with emotion. Frank took a deep breath, his eyes softening as he realized the truth in her words. "I'm proud of you, Annie. I just don't want to lose the woman I fell in love with in the process."

With that conversation, they made a pact to prioritize their relationship amidst the chaos. They began to communicate more openly, sharing their fears and dreams, and setting aside time for each other, no matter how busy their schedules became. This newfound commitment brought them closer together, strengthening their bond and allowing them to face the challenges of fame as a united front.

As the months passed, Annie and Frank found a rhythm that allowed them to balance their personal and professional lives. They embraced the chaos of the Wild West Show while also nurturing their love, creating a beautiful harmony that resonated in both their performances and their private moments. Their shared experiences on the road became the foundation of their relationship, and they learned to lean on each other during the highs and lows of their journey.

Annie's fame continued to grow, and with it came opportunities that would take her to new heights. She was invited to perform for dignitaries and celebrities, and her name became synonymous with excellence in sharpshooting. Yet, amidst the glamour and excitement, she remained grounded, always returning to the love and support of Frank. They would often reminisce about their early days, laughing at the memories of their first competitions and the spark that ignited their romance.

One summer, they decided to take a much-needed break from the stage and embarked on a road trip across the country. With their wagon packed and the open road ahead, they set off on an adventure that would allow them to reconnect with each other and the world around them. They visited national parks, explored small towns, and met fellow travelers who shared their passion for shooting and adventure. Each stop along the way was an opportunity to create new memories, and they cherished the time spent together, free from the pressures of performance.

During their travels, Annie also took the time to reflect on her role as a pioneer for women in sports. She began to understand the impact of her journey not just on her own life but on the lives of countless others. Inspired by the stories of young girls who looked up to her, she decided to host shooting clinics in various towns they visited. These clinics became a way for her to give back, empowering young women to embrace their passions and break free from societal expectations. Frank stood by her side, helping to organize the events and cheering on the participants as they took their first shots.

As the couple continued to travel and share their love for shooting, they also faced the inevitable challenges that come with fame. Rumors and speculation about their personal lives began to swirl, and the couple found themselves under the scrutiny of the public eye. Annie remained steadfast in her commitment to authenticity, refusing to let the gossip affect her relationship with Frank. They learned to navigate the challenges together, using humor and open communication to strengthen their bond.

One evening, after a particularly challenging day filled with media attention, Annie and Frank found solace in a quiet moment under the stars. "You know, no matter what they say, I know who you are," Frank said, wrapping his arm around her. "You're my partner, my love, and that's all that matters." Annie smiled, feeling a wave of gratitude wash over her. "And you're mine, Frank. Together, we can face anything."

As they continued to build their life together, Annie and Frank also dreamed of starting a family. They envisioned a future filled with laughter, love, and the joy of sharing their passions with the next generation. However, the demands of their careers often made it difficult to find the right time to start a family. They navigated this uncertainty with grace, supporting each other's dreams while remaining hopeful for what the future would hold.

In the midst of their busy lives, Annie also took the time to explore her own interests outside of shooting. She developed a love for writing, often penning her thoughts and experiences in a journal. This creative outlet allowed her to express herself in new ways and provided a sense of clarity amidst the chaos. Frank encouraged her to share her stories, and together they began to explore the idea of publishing a book that would inspire others to pursue their passions.

ADVOCACY AND IMPACT

As Annie Oakley continued to dazzle audiences around the world with her extraordinary sharpshooting skills, she recognized that her influence extended far beyond the stage. The roar of the crowd echoed in her ears, but it was the whispers of young girls and women who looked up to her that ignited a fire within her heart. Annie understood that she had become a symbol of empowerment and possibility, and she was determined to use her platform to advocate for women's rights, education, and the responsible use of firearms.

Her journey into advocacy began during one of the Wild West Show's performances in a small town in the Midwest. After the show, a group of young girls approached her, their eyes wide with admiration. They asked her questions about her life, her skills, and how they could become sharpshooters like her. As Annie spoke with them, she felt a profound sense of responsibility. These girls, filled with dreams and aspirations, saw her not just as a performer but as a role model. It was in that moment that she realized the impact she could have on their lives.

Determined to inspire and empower the next generation, Annie began organizing shooting clinics for young girls across the country. These clinics were not just about marksmanship; they were about instilling confidence, resilience, and the belief that they could achieve anything they set their minds to. Annie's infectious enthusiasm and genuine passion for teaching drew participants from all walks of life, and the events quickly became a celebration of empowerment.

The clinics were filled with laughter, camaraderie, and the thrill of learning. Annie would share her own experiences, recounting stories of her journey from a young girl in Ohio to a world-renowned sharpshooter. She encouraged the girls to embrace their individuality and pursue their passions unapologetically. "You are capable of greatness," she would tell them, her eyes sparkling with conviction. "Don't let anyone tell you otherwise."

As the clinics gained popularity, Annie's advocacy began to attract attention from local newspapers and women's organizations. She was invited to speak at events, sharing her vision for a world where women could pursue their dreams without limitations. Her speeches were filled with passion and purpose, resonating with audiences who were eager to hear her message of empowerment. "Women belong in every arena," she declared, her voice unwavering. "Whether it's the shooting range, the boardroom, or the stage, we have the right to excel."

Annie's advocacy extended beyond the realm of shooting. She became an outspoken supporter of women's suffrage, recognizing that the fight for equal rights was intertwined with her own journey. She attended rallies and events, lending her voice to the cause and encouraging others to join the movement. Her presence at these gatherings was electrifying; she embodied the spirit of determination that fueled the suffrage movement. "We are not just fighting for our rights; we are fighting for the rights of future generations," she proclaimed, inspiring those around her to take action.

In 1896, Annie was invited to speak at a national women's rights convention in Washington, D.C. The event was a pivotal moment in her advocacy journey. Standing before a crowd of passionate activists, she felt a surge of energy and purpose. As she took the stage, she could see the faces of women from all walks of life, united in their quest for equality. With each word she spoke, she felt the weight of history on her shoulders, and she knew that her voice could make a difference.

"Women have the right to choose their own paths, to pursue their passions, and to have their voices heard," she declared, her voice ringing with conviction. "We must break the chains of societal expectations and forge our destinies." The audience erupted in applause, and Annie felt a rush of exhilaration. In that moment, she realized that her advocacy was not just about her own journey; it was about uplifting others and creating a future where women could thrive.

As her reputation as an advocate grew, Annie also became involved in promoting responsible gun ownership. She believed that with great power came great responsibility, and she wanted to ensure that the next generation understood the importance of safety and respect when it came to firearms. She collaborated with local organizations to host workshops that educated young shooters on proper handling, safety protocols, and the ethical use of firearms. These workshops were designed to empower participants, teaching them that being a skilled shooter came with the duty to act responsibly.

Annie's commitment to advocacy did not go unnoticed. She received numerous accolades and recognition for her efforts, including invitations to join prominent women's organizations and speak at influential gatherings. However, she remained humble, always redirecting the spotlight to the cause she championed. "It's not about me," she would say. "It's about the women who come after us, the girls who will one day take the stage and make their own mark on the world."

With Frank by her side, Annie traveled across the country, attending events and speaking engagements. Their partnership became a powerful force for change, and together they inspired countless individuals to embrace their passions and advocate for their rights. Frank, who had always been her steadfast supporter, took on a more active role in her advocacy efforts, helping to organize events and manage logistics. Their shared vision for a more equitable world fueled their commitment, and they became a dynamic duo in the fight for women's empowerment.

One of the most memorable events they organized was a national shooting competition for women, designed to showcase female talent and promote camaraderie among participants. The event attracted women from all over the country, each eager to demonstrate their skills and connect with like-minded individuals. Annie's presence at the competition was electrifying; she not only participated but also mentored the contestants, offering guidance and encouragement. "This is your moment to shine," she told them, her voice filled with warmth. "Show the world what you're capable of."

The competition was a resounding success, drawing media attention and sparking conversations about women in sports. Annie's advocacy efforts were making waves, and she was increasingly recognized as a leader in the movement for women's rights. However, she remained grounded, always reminding herself of the young girls who inspired her to take action in the first place.

As Annie's influence grew, she began to receive invitations to collaborate with other prominent figures in the women's rights movement. She joined forces with suffragists, educators, and activists, working together to create initiatives that would empower women in various fields. Annie's ability to connect with people from all walks of life made her a sought-after speaker, and she used her platform to amplify the voices of those who were often overlooked.

In her speeches, Annie often shared personal anecdotes that resonated with her audience. She spoke of her own struggles and triumphs, emphasizing the importance of perseverance and self-belief. "Every challenge I faced only made me stronger," she would say, her eyes shining with determination. "And I want you to know that you have the strength within you to overcome any obstacle."

Annie's advocacy also extended to education, as she believed that knowledge was a powerful tool for empowerment. She partnered with local schools to promote programs that encouraged girls to pursue education in fields traditionally dominated by men, such as science, technology, engineering, and mathematics (STEM). She organized workshops and mentorship programs, inviting successful women from various professions to share their stories and inspire the next generation.

Through her efforts, Annie helped to create a network of support for young women, fostering an environment where they could thrive and pursue their dreams without fear of judgment. She often reminded them, "You are the architects of your own futures. Build them with courage and conviction."

As the years went by, Annie's impact continued to grow, and she became a beloved figure not only in the world of sharpshooting but also in the broader movement for women's rights. Her legacy was one of empowerment, resilience, and unwavering commitment to creating a better world for future generations. She inspired countless women to take up arms—not just in the literal sense of shooting but in the fight for their rights and the pursuit of their passions.

LATER YEARS AND LEGACY

As the sun dipped below the horizon, casting a warm glow over the landscape, Annie Oakley sat on the porch of her modest home in North Carolina, reflecting on a life filled with adventure, advocacy, and achievement. The applause of countless audiences faded into memory, but the impact she had made on the world remained vibrant and alive. In her later years, Annie embraced a new chapter, one that would allow her to solidify her legacy and inspire future generations.

The years following her peak in the spotlight were not without their challenges. The world was changing rapidly, and with it came new social dynamics and expectations. Annie found herself navigating the complexities of fame while striving to maintain a sense of normalcy in her personal life. The pressures of public life had taken their toll, but she remained resolute in her commitment to her causes and the people who looked up to her.

In the early 1900s, Annie began to focus her efforts on education, particularly for young girls interested in pursuing careers in sports and other male-dominated fields. She established scholarships to support their education and partnered with local schools to promote physical education programs that included shooting and archery. "Every girl deserves the chance to discover her potential," she would say, her voice filled with conviction. "Education is the key that unlocks the door to opportunity."

Annie's work in education was transformative. She traveled across the country, speaking at schools and community centers, igniting a passion for learning and self-improvement in young women. Her workshops were not just about shooting; they were about building confidence, resilience, and a sense of belonging. She encouraged her students to embrace their individuality and pursue their dreams, no matter how unconventional they might seem. "You are capable of greatness," she would tell them, her eyes shining with encouragement. "Never let anyone tell you otherwise."

In 1903, Annie was invited to participate in the World's Fair in St. Louis, a grand event that showcased the latest innovations and cultural achievements of the time. It was an opportunity for her to demonstrate her skills on an international stage and to advocate for women in sports. The fair was filled with excitement and wonder, and Annie seized the moment to inspire others. She set up a shooting exhibition that drew crowds from all over the world, captivating audiences with her precision and flair.

But beyond the spectacle of her performances, Annie used the platform to address the importance of women's rights and empowerment. She delivered speeches that resonated deeply with the audience, emphasizing the need for equality in all aspects of life. "This is not just about shooting; it's about breaking down barriers and proving that women can excel in any field," she declared, her voice resonating with passion. The crowd erupted in applause, and Annie felt the energy of the moment, knowing she was making a difference.

As the years passed, Annie's health began to decline. She faced various challenges, including a serious illness that forced her to step back from performing. Yet, even during her struggles, her spirit remained unbroken. She continued to advocate for her causes, using her voice to raise awareness about the importance of health care and support for those facing similar battles. "Life may throw challenges our way, but we must rise to meet them with courage and determination," she would remind her supporters.

In her later years, Annie also turned her attention to writing. She began to pen her memoirs, recounting the stories of her life, the lessons she had learned, and the people who had inspired her along the way. The act of writing became a cathartic experience, allowing her to reflect on her journey and share her wisdom with others. "I want my story to inspire young women to chase their dreams," she wrote in her journal. "Every challenge I faced only made me stronger, and I hope they see that they too can overcome anything."

Annie's memoirs became a powerful tool for advocacy, and she sought to publish them as a way to reach a wider audience. She envisioned a book that would not only tell her story but also serve as a guide for young women navigating their own paths. "This is more than just my story; it's a testament to the strength of women everywhere," she wrote, her heart filled with hope.

Despite the challenges she faced, Annie remained a beacon of light for those around her. Her home became a gathering place for activists, educators, and young women eager to learn from her experiences. She welcomed them with open arms, sharing her knowledge and encouraging them to pursue their passions. "Together, we can create a world where women are empowered to follow their dreams," she would say, her voice unwavering.

As her health continued to decline, Annie found solace in her relationships with family and friends. Frank remained her steadfast partner, supporting her through every challenge. Their love had weathered the storms of fame and adversity, and they found comfort in each other's presence. "You are my rock, Frank," Annie would say, her eyes filled with gratitude. " Together, we have built a legacy that will inspire generations to come." Their bond was a testament to the power of love and partnership, and it fueled Annie's determination to leave a lasting impact on the world.

In the twilight of her life, Annie Oakley became a symbol of resilience and empowerment. She continued to advocate for women's rights, using her voice to speak out against injustices and to promote equality. Her speeches resonated with audiences, reminding them of the importance of standing up for what is right. "We must never forget that our fight is not just for ourselves but for all women who come after us," she would declare, her voice strong and unwavering.

Annie's legacy extended far beyond her remarkable sharpshooting skills. She had become a pioneer for women in sports, a champion for education, and a fierce advocate for equality. Her influence was felt not only in the world of marksmanship but also in the hearts of those she inspired.

Young women across the country looked to her as a role model, drawing strength from her story and her unwavering belief in their potential.

As she neared the end of her journey, Annie reflected on the impact she had made. She had faced challenges, overcome obstacles, and inspired countless individuals to pursue their dreams. "I may be just one woman, but I have always believed in the power of one voice to create change," she wrote in her memoirs. "If I can inspire even one person to chase their dreams, then my life has been worth it."

Annie Oakley passed away on November 3, 1926, leaving behind a legacy that would endure for generations. Her contributions to women's rights, education, and sports paved the way for future trailblazers. In the years that followed, her story continued to inspire countless individuals, reminding them of the importance of perseverance, courage, and the belief that they could achieve anything they set their minds to.

Today, Annie's legacy lives on in the hearts of those who continue to fight for equality and empowerment. Her story is taught in schools, celebrated in literature, and honored in various forms of media. She is remembered not only as a sharpshooter but as a pioneer who broke barriers and inspired a movement.

In the end, Annie Oakley's life was a testament to the power of passion, determination, and the unwavering belief in one's potential. Her journey from a small-town girl to a global icon serves as a reminder that with courage and conviction, anyone can make a difference. As the sun sets on her remarkable story, it rises anew in the hearts of those who carry her legacy forward, ensuring that her impact will never be forgotten.

WRAP-UP

The story of Annie Oakley is one of remarkable resilience, unwavering determination, and the relentless pursuit of dreams. From her humble beginnings in rural Ohio to becoming one of the most celebrated sharpshooters in history, Annie's journey transcends the boundaries of her time, marking her as a trailblazer for women everywhere. Her legacy is not merely defined by her extraordinary marksmanship but by the powerful message she championed: that women have the right to carve their own paths and pursue their passions without limitation.

Annie's life was a tapestry of triumphs and challenges, woven together by her unyielding spirit. She broke through societal norms, proving that women could excel in fields traditionally dominated by men. Her advocacy for women's rights and education laid the groundwork for future generations, inspiring countless young girls to embrace their ambitions and defy expectations. Through her shooting clinics, public speeches, and unwavering support for the suffrage movement, Annie became a voice for those who had been silenced, igniting a flame of empowerment that continues to burn brightly today.

Even in her later years, as she faced health challenges and the inevitable passage of time, Annie remained committed to her causes. She became a mentor, a teacher, and a beacon of hope for those who sought guidance. Her memoirs, filled with wisdom and personal anecdotes, serve as a testament to her belief in the transformative power of education and self-discovery. Annie understood that her story was not just her own; it was a collective narrative that resonated with the dreams and aspirations of women everywhere.

Annie Oakley's spirit endures in the hearts of those she inspired. Her legacy is celebrated in museums, literature, and educational programs, reminding us of the importance of perseverance and the strength that lies within each of us. She is a symbol of empowerment, a reminder that every individual has the capacity to create change, challenge the status quo, and make a lasting impact on the world.

As we reflect on Annie's life, we are reminded that her journey is far from over. Each time a young girl picks up a rifle, a woman advocates for her rights, or someone dares to dream beyond societal expectations, Annie's spirit lives on. Her story continues to inspire new generations to pursue their passions fearlessly, to stand up for their beliefs, and to embrace the power of their voices.

In a world that often seeks to define us by limitations, Annie Oakley's legacy serves as a clarion call to break free from those constraints. She teaches us that with courage, resilience, and a commitment to our dreams, we can overcome any obstacle and leave an indelible mark on the world. The enduring spirit of Annie Oakley reminds us that we are all capable of greatness, and that our stories, like hers, have the power to inspire change and uplift those around us.

In the end, Annie Oakley is not just a historical figure; she is a symbol of hope, empowerment, and the relentless pursuit of dreams. Her legacy will continue to inspire, challenge, and uplift those who dare to follow in her footsteps, ensuring that her spirit remains alive for generations to come.

Printed in Great Britain
by Amazon